Something Like a Life

Poems

Sally Zakariya

Gyroscope Press

This publication is a creative work protected in full by all applicable copyright laws. No part of this book may be reproduced or transmitted in any form or by any means, electronic or mechanical, including photocopying, recording, or by any information storage and retrieval system without the written permission of Gyroscope Press, except in the case of brief quotations embodied in critical articles or reviews or where permitted by law. All rights reserved.

Gyroscope Press
PO Box 1989
Gillette, WY 82717
gyroscopepress@gmail.com

Something Like a Life
Copyright © 2021 by Sally Zakariya
First Edition 2021

Cover Photo by Sally Zakariya
Cover Design, Interior Layout by Constance Brewer

ISBN: 9781736782019

Published in the United States of America

For my parents, in memory

Contents

Father's Day 9
Made of Song 10
Genealogy 12
Maine Ghosts, 1952 13
Between the Words 14
How It Is for Us 16
Photograph of My Son 17
Storm in Hawai'i 18
Between Possibilities 20
What I Know about Chemistry 21
The Things He Left 22
Walnut Hill 23
Ode to Trash 24
Hearing Father Read 'The Turn of the Screw' 25
Grace Notes 26
Wedding Party 27
Photograph of My Grandfather 28
November 1963 29
The Written Word 30
That Long Quiet 32
Winter Can Wait 34
Free Flight 35
Junior Altar Guild 36
Mother Whistling in Heaven 38

Edison Street Excavation 39
Cathedral Lament 40
Rounding 65..41
Since Last Wednesday...42
Making a Life..43
Between Me and the Finish Line 44
Acknowledgments...45
About the Author...46

Something Like a Life

Father's Day

Tubby's Place he called it
the restaurant he dreamed
of someday starting

Already round as a young man
and never lost that baby fat
already turning jokes against himself
so he could be the first to do so
no doubt already seeing
a life of corpulence ahead

He sang and whistled
and told funny stories
but anger derailed him
with its sudden storms
and then there was despair
and all the bad health
that comes with weight

In his last photo he stands
against a rail fence somewhere
in Virginia, face and belly
circle on circle like the
how-to-draw books show
thinning hair suddenly white
legs stolidly spread as though
loath to relinquish the ground
he has claimed

Made of Song

I wanted to be made of the song that was in your
    head

the cape of music loose around your shoulders
white hot with harmony
fingers drumming the car roof
blazing down the skyway in our
old Plymouth

You would sing me into sleep
drifting into the song
dreaming into it
waking into a lazy beat

Sometimes you sang "froggie went a'courting"
sometimes old English ballads
sometimes the anger song, a song I recognized

I remember the words

Wherever the music went, you went with it, or you
    took it
when you left, or the song in your head went silent

I would climb the chokecherry tree and sit
where the big branch angled out of the trunk
folded in a lazy V, reading a book

listening for a song that might have been in my head
if not in yours

wanting wings like the birds who ate the berries and
    sang
like they were made of song

Genealogy

Grandma was the second wife,
good hearty German stock.
The first wife perished young
with her two infant sons when
influenza swept the city.

We'd heard of her—Miss
Lillian—but not the babies,
those little half-brothers
my father never knew, never
even knew existed.

It took a curious cousin
with a research bent
to discover them, to find
their death certificates
and their tiny graves.

Who would they have been?
Weathermen like Uncle Bill?
Soldiers like Uncle George?
Librarians like father?
I'd like to think someone

somewhere keeps a list
of all the little ones who
didn't make it, what they
wanted, what they loved,
what they hoped to give.

Maine Ghosts, 1952

A knob-kneed moose comes quietly at dawn to
 browse
the tender plants in the garden next door, tilting
the broad bowl of his antlers.

It's the closest I've been to the wild. We've driven up
to Maine in the old Plymouth, Daddy singing, Mother
 fretting,
we kids squabbling in back.

The pond calms us with placid waters. We jump
feet first from the dock, hair fanning like brush
 strokes
on a watercolor morning.

Later, sun shimmering around us, we row out from
 shore
to the smooth belly of the pond. Big-eyed dragonflies
skim the surface with glassy wings.

We recite the litany of trees that rim the shore: alder,
 ash, black
willow, paper birch—what the Penobscot used for
 their canoes,
root lashed, slender, swift.

At night the loon's staccato cry brings those first
 people back
to almost life, slipping silent through woods where no
 cabins
stand, gliding half-seen in birch bark canoes.

Between the Words

Nature has the last word,
always does, so when I send
you a message in a bottle,
the sea scrubs the ink off
the paper, and when the bottle
washes up ashore, the sand
welcomes a long-lost
brother, somehow evolved
into glass without the hell
of the furnace

And when I sing a song
for you in my old voice,
cracked and off key,
a blustery breeze
blows the tune away,
and finches drown
me out with their own
avian halleluiah
chorus, praising sun
and seeds and airy
acrobatics

So instead I write you
a poem with imaginary
spaces between each word,
spaces so deep and wide

there's room for both of us,
and as you read, the clock
ticks slowly — so slowly
nature's daily round
will seem to last
forever

How It Is for Us

How you recline, old man odalisque on the couch
head back ... legs crossed ... shirt hiked up to show
an inch or two of belly

How we trade rants and outrages as we read the
    news
Post for you, *Times* for me and then reverse ... you
    sailing
your paper to me edge forward like a flying wing, me
frisbeeing mine folded but falling short

How the sun slants in through curtains caught
in claws two cats ago, each fold of sheer gray stuff
casting oblique shadows on the ceiling ... drawing
my eye to the corner cobweb

How the coffee cools in the old pottery mugs
from the farmer's market ... sweet dregs
clotting dark at the bottom

This is how it is for us, our little ritual or one
of them, along with regular long drives to no place
in particular ... sharing rice pudding at the Greek
diner ... watching PBS and worse at night

you playing your odalisque role and me feet
up on the cat-scratched ottoman ... how it is
for us is good, and also for the cats

Photograph of My Son

The picture in the paper
looks like my son but younger
before his hair began to go
before determined cycling
built his muscles so hard
all those miles away.

I cut the picture out
talk to it, to my dear son
flat and thin and young.

He is about to speak.
I miss you he says.

Or is that what I say
to the picture that is
and is not my son.

Storm in Hawai'i

> *Home is the place where, when you have to go there,*
> *they have to take you in.* —Robert Frost

So long away, he has come home again
to visit the family he hasn't seen
for 15 years.

The wayward son, the son who disappoints,
the son who wouldn't follow the path,
take on the yoke of 9 to 5.

He sits on the rocks where that morning
they watched whales breach free, exultant,
through the waves.

But a storm is brewing, or else the father
calls one up from the Pacific,
summoning its wrath.

"If you have kids," the father fumes,
"I hope they're just as ungrateful
as you have been."

It's a malediction out of nowhere. "Jesus,"
he thinks, "but hey, I know how harsh
the old man can be."

"Home is the place where when I look for it,"
he thinks, "I can't find it anywhere."

He sees the darkening moon sink slowly
into the sea, dragging tattered clouds down
into the roiling waves.

Between Possibilities

We live between possibilities
you like to say
between the likely paths
we could have followed
this way or that

actors between
engagements
shaking off the cloaks
of past characters
chasing new roles
new souls to inhabit

fields between seasons
dead stalks bent sharply
to the ground before
the first hint of green
pushes through

held in stasis in the
spaces we have built
we stay at home
in our in between

What I Know about Chemistry

Grandfather was a chemist but the science
gene died with him in the Maine woods.

Hiker, archer, fisherman, consummate
outdoorsman, but still always a chemist

pursuing the central science. I see
him white coated with his test tubes

exploring the essential secrets
of the universe, matter's mysteries

how atoms meet and dance and bond
in shapely mathematical precision.

I can't fathom such formidable beauty
can't grasp the fundamental knowledge

he held so easily. Did he see molecules
in dreams, devise arcane reactions as he

walked from home to lab, from lab to home?
Samuel Stockton Voorhees—I look in vain

for some suggestion of his sibilant name
in the periodic table. But never mind.

When he was young, I'm told, he saved a man
from drowning in the Johnstown Flood

no doubt analyzing the murky mixture
of flood water and debris as he dove in.

The Things He Left

Book, mostly, history, politics, and classics
the real classics, Latin and Greek—
he taught them years ago to privileged
prep school boys in Tennessee and still
read Cicero and Horace in the cafeteria
at lunch, or so his colleagues told us
    when he died

Also handwritten recipes copied from old
Gourmet magazines—dishes he wouldn't make
but savored in contemplation while he ate
his corned beef sandwich, imagining perhaps
    a Roman banquet

And Southern blues and jazz on brittle black
discs, music of his childhood and mine
Bessie Smith, King Oliver, Lead Belly
    music in the names

He left friends at the deli, carpool and library
mates, cocktail parties where he beguiled guests
with his stories and his laugh—and once swigged
jiggers of maple syrup when the whiskey
    ran low

He left early, before his time, left us three
Mother, sister, me, lost in our own
    quiet blues

Walnut Hill

Memphis summer. Air so still
that just to breathe tips an uneasy
scale of heat and haze.

I walk up the dusty drive, walnuts
crunching underfoot. Nameless insects
rasp a busy chorus.

The big house sits empty on a slight rise
the once grand property shrunk to two
square blocks, railroad on one side,
suburb on the other.

From here the family patriarch crossed
the Mississippi to coax cotton
from the rich red earth.

From here the woman whose name I bear
traveled through battlegrounds in a hired boxcar
taking piano and slave to a Georgia college
while the war still raged.

From here generations of us have come
bearing the weight of that dark history.

All gone now—gone with the cotton money,
gone with the plantation dreams and myths.
I peer in a window and see dust motes
dance in the slanting sun like guests
at the elegant parties held by the last owner—
a Black man.

Ode to Trash

Something like a life
spills from the bin
breakfast egg shells
yesterday's junk mail
a torn glove and its mate
worthless alone
like many of us

We have the capacity
to love entirely, even
bits and pieces we've
discarded—outdated,
unneeded, unwanted
until it's too late

Love is a process of loss
the off-hand *see you*
the tossed-out letters
the distance from the other
the final farewell

I take out the trash unsure
the bin is big enough
to hold it all—all the debris
and detritus, the mistakes
and missteps, unsure
if I can live without
what I've cast away

Hearing Father Read 'The Turn of the Screw'

My friend and I home from college, my father
surprises us by reading the story aloud

his Southern voice at once both soft and deep
not at all a Henry James sort of voice

the voice of someone who has known ghosts
of his own and is wary reading about them.

A succession of flights and drops ... that's how
the governess begins her melancholy tale.

What nature of evil Miles and Flora face
out by the lake we can only imagine, safe

as we are in our suburban house, windows open
curtains sighing with each breath of breeze

the old dog (it was Skipper then) a ball of black
and white curled at my feet while mother washes up

missing the unfolding ambiguities, the undertones
and veiled suggestions, the final sadness.

Grace Notes

It's so much work to stay alive
but living has its payoffs
> *sunset so stunning it burns your eyes*
> *mathematical precision in a seashell*
> *an unexpected kind word*
> *in a foreign city*

not that any of these will fix
the human condition
> *after all there's a graveyard*
> *beneath everything*

but such small grace notes
can lighten the load

Like when you teared up
kissing that girl good-bye
in the Yugoslav train station
all those years ago and the men
nearby wiped their eyes as well
and patted your shoulder
in solidarity—no matter
you shared no language
no lived experience, you
a U.S. vagabond surrounded
by Slovenian workers

The station was shabby, squalid
yet the memory of their kindness
lifts your spirits still

Wedding Party

Growing up I only knew three Black people
in the whole of Virginia

>	Dolores, who cleaned our house in a casual
>	sort of way and drank my Daddy's bourbon
>	until he locked it up
>
>	Whip-thin Eunice, who cleaned with grit
>	and energy and laughed when Mother shrieked
>	at the rat that ran out of the basement john
>
>	Curtis, her handsome husband who spoke
>	the king's English with a Caribbean lilt
>	and had a hot pink Cadillac convertible

He drove my sister to the church in that car
on her wedding day, she in the filmy white
dress we had just finished hemming
sitting tailor style with Mother on the
double bed and handing the skirt around
in a kind of fairy circle but with needles

People were shocked when they saw the two
drive up with the top down—his skin so shiny
black, her dress so innocent white,
the car pink as cotton candy

It was Virginia, did I say

Photograph of My Grandfather

Man with a brush mustache
standing straight and tall and lean
like the birch trees behind him,
in one hand a fishing rod
in the other a string
of yellow perch.

Above,
jays wheel and soar.

Around,
shrubs and brambles
tangle his feet.

Ahead,
stands the old friend
who carved a bow for him,
who showed him the spot
where fish leapt at the bait,
who took the photograph,
who tried in vain to get him
to the hospital in time
when his appendix burst
there in the Maine woods.

November 1963

For my father, 1910-1963

I'm watching the riderless black horse at JFK's funeral
when the call comes. *Try to be strong for your mother*
they say, but who will be strong for you lying silent
and still in the hospital bed with tentacle tubes
screen blinking like the black-and-white TV
I was watching, adjusting the rabbit ears to get
a better picture.

There is no better picture of you, not now.
There is a three-day stubble on your chin as though
you finally decided to grow a beard below that bristly
grey moustache and your belly rises like a burial
mound beneath its sheet and your breath
is heavy with dread.

Thanksgiving comes, the women
bake, the family gathers, but what do we have
to give thanks for. There is no black horse
for you at the end.

The Written Word

For my mother, 1907-1980

After we were tucked in
after she settled her mother
for the night, brushing the long white hair
setting the silver bell by her bedside
after she let Dusty out in the yard
and then back in

After that my mother would retreat
into words, novel open
cigarettes at hand

Or she'd take the Smith Corona
to the bathroom and send
crisp black letters across the page
each keystroke pinning words on paper
like insects in a specimen case

With the spoken word
she was less forthcoming
dinnertime debates would drive her from the room
some things (she said) a well-bred person
simply doesn't speak of
money for one or sickness or politics or feelings
or Great Aunt Sarah's disastrous marriage

The many things she never
told me would fill pages
what it was like to be an afterthought

third girl years later, not the son they hoped for
what it was like to lose the man before her husband
the man who gave her the small figure
of a fox she so treasured
what it was like to try
and fail at a life on stage
speaking someone else's
written words

That Long Quiet

She died at home but in the wrong room
at home the way she wanted but not
her own room

Silent in the rented hospital bed
perhaps she sensed it coming
that long quiet

Roast beef on Sunday and peach skillet
pie her practical legacy and also how
to darn a sock

Other legacies were less tangible
the way to know birds by their songs
the reading habit

the mannerly exterior, but still
there was plenty none of us
got right

She heard it coming, didn't she
heard the quiet come up and wrap
itself around her

The nurse was there that last day
but I wasn't, I didn't even
get that right

No longer her house, the draperies
gone, the wall-to-wall, the Chinese
figured paper

Everything changed and rearranged
but still quiet, and still I'm not sure
I got it right

Winter Can Wait

A leaf falls, floats
others follow it down
to gather on the ground

But oak leaves are stubborn
hanging on through rain
and snow, no longer green
and smooth, growing dry
and crisp, rustling gently
in the wind, in no hurry
to join the others
on the ground

Like you, thank God

Heart out of sync, sugar
in the blood, a little crab
gnawing inside until
they caught it, and you
hanging on, in no hurry
to reach the ground

Spring and summer
done, autumn ongoing
winter can wait

Free Flight

> *"Silent Magic is a fair description of rubber powered model airplane flight."* —Don Ross, *Rubber Powered Model Airplanes*

First build an ethereal
geometry of flight—
balsa wood and tissue paper
no plastic or paint or decals
no growling motors
just rubber bands
to power ascent

Dragonfly propeller
wind-raked wings
soaring against the sun
a sense of negative weight
drawn on the air

A moment or two
of seeming stasis
before the inevitable
plummet downward
to be left where it falls
tangled in trees

And then the urge
to build again
to create and let fly
to put a frame around
a personal slice
of eternity

Junior Altar Guild

St. George's Church—I get to trim
tall glads and stand them in bronzy
vases that have ears for handles
and take them to our chapel while
the ladies' guild does the honors
in the church itself.

I expect God has better things to do
than watch if I make a proper bow
at the altar but I'm not taking chances—
not at 13 with adolescent yearning in
full melodrama bloom and that thrilling
thirst for piety.

I smooth an altar cloth that needs no
smoothing, in touch somehow with
the sublime, the central figure in my own
passion play. The organist is practicing,
plump fingers pumping out "Sheep
May Safely Graze."

We sing at the cathedral, the mixed
voices of our massed choir carried
on the glorious exhalations of organ
pipes from choir stalls small as dwarf
furniture under the soaring
spears of stone.

The light through leaded windows
tells stories of the martyrs in bright glass

colored inside the lines. But it's
the catacombs that matter in the end
the catacombs that catch the angels
when they fall, amazed.

Mother Whistling in Heaven

Thrifty in everything except your love
for the parade of dogs who walked

at your heel—Dusty, Skipper, Finnegan—
good dogs, they came when you whistled

and so did we until the mockingbird learned
to whistle too, a lesson in bird song and

who you can trust. You taught us how
to know trees and wildflowers and how

to can tomatoes and peaches and store them
on the dim shelves under the basement stairs.

Depression-schooled, you turned sheets
top to bottom and sewed us party dresses

out of parachute silk brought back from
Japan by Uncle Ralph and dyed rose pink.

And if they joined you in your heaven, those
Japanese pilots the silk was meant to save,

they would drift, bowing, into your
billowy pink cloud. No more war now,

no more making do, just smoking cigarettes,
playing bridge, whistling for the dogs.

Edison Street Excavation

They couldn't leave the farm behind
when they moved to our block
the whole unruly lot of them—
aunts uncles cousins
     coming and going
          coupling and uncoupling
and always clinging to them
the memory of the plow

It was a post-war suburb
     square faceless brick
          perfunctory lawns
but on an extra lot they grew
corn and beans and grapes
and built a shed
     one side for chickens
          the other for a mule

The youngest girl and I played forts
and fantasies in the brambles by the tracks
that traced their plot   a daily train
     clattering by at 5 o'clock
          rousing the dogs
telling us day was running down

Still the hint of fields hovers somehow
in the air   the almost smell of dry straw
     faint scratch of chickens
          bramble's prickle
on a child's remembered shin

Cathedral Lament

Served a whole fish on a dinner plate
in a restaurant in Southern France,
I put a piece of lettuce on its head
to hide its accusing eye.

The waiter laughed, but my mind was elsewhere,
caught out of nowhere with a sudden sense
of loss—an idea of children I might have had,
blind potential swimming in the dark.

We'd been to the Cathedrale de la Major
with its Byzantine domes, its tombs of saints,
its chapel of the Virgin and graceful Pieta,
its heavy load of awe and guilt.

Outside, in bright sun and breeze that hinted
of the sea, I bought an angel painted
on a wooden panel, icon-style, with golden
wings and all the Catholic trappings.

That night as the clangor of bells echoed
through the streets, I dreamed of babies
who never were, of a loss that never was.
I woke to an accusing angel's eye.

Rounding 65

Even old I'll hold you he says
as we round 65 and head for 70
I'll remember the words you forget
carry the heavy grocery bags
change light bulbs that are too high
    to reach

And I'll speak up as your hearing dims
I tell him and handle your email
and tuck the label back inside
the neck of your shirt as if
    it mattered

We'll finish each other's sentences
bring donuts if we're feeling poorly
ignore our bodies' indecorous sounds
    and degradation

Forty-some birthdays and anniversaries
we've given all the gifts we need
giving now what matters most—
the promise to hold on

Since Last Wednesday

The world has gone on
the wheels turned
lives began and ended
birds announced the morning
again and again
as though nothing changed
as though no blind
cleaver had cut last
Wednesday from all
days before or after
and left it standing
alone somewhere
sidelined as the great
spiral took the rest
of us on its relentless way
sightseers in time
and space but without
you along to share
the ride

Making a Life

We make a life in the old brick house
we two, then three

We say the words at the courthouse
and this new life begins
made of work and food and diapers
    and dust under the bed
made of talk and silence, of touch and glance
of love, whatever that means

It means remembering and forgetting
    and being angry
and then sad and then laughing

It means sharing and giving
    and scraping by
when there isn't really enough

It means building a life, patching the cracks
    painting the woodwork
and making room for more

It means holding things together while we make
that life, while we find comfort in each other
    we two, then three

Between Me and the Finish Line

It's not like I'm racing to the finish line—
the line and I will meet in our own good time,
and I give little thought to what might
happen next.

No, it's all the stuff crowding the space ahead
that worries me—all the necessary business
and blues, all the jumbled memes and memories,
all the day-to-day trivialities to get through before
I cross that line.

How many trips to the grocery store, how many
poems started and abandoned, how many
dreams deferred beyond hope? Wash my face,
wash the dishes, wash the clothes. Wash my
soul if it's not too late, if there's still time,
still space between me and the finish line.

Sometimes fear wraps its fist around me
as I survey the dwindling distance,
the waning chance of anything
like transcendence.

But sometimes you don't know quite
what you're looking for, and sometimes
you don't really know who you are until
you realize you've found it.

Acknowledgments

I am grateful to the following publications, in which these poems appeared, sometimes in slightly different forms:

Between the Lines: Walnut Hill, Issue 3, 2016
Boston Literary Magazine: What I Know about Chemistry, Winter 2013-14
Broadkill Review: Maine Ghosts, 1952, November/December 2014
Burningword Literary Journal: Grace Notes, October 2020
Connecticut River Review: That Long Quiet, 2014
Edge: Since Last Wednesday, Volume 8, 2014
Fredericksburg Literary Review: Edison Street Excavation, Fall 2015
Muslim Wife (Blue Lyra Press Delphi Series, Volume 7 (2019): Between the Words
Poetry South: The Things He Left, 2016
The Poeming Pigeon: Love Poems, Rounding 65, 2017
Third Wednesday: Made Out of Song and Wedding Party, Summer 2013

About the Author

Sally Zakariya's poetry has appeared in some 75 print and online journals and been nominated for the Pushcart Prize and Best of the Net. Her most recent publication is *Muslim Wife* (Blue Lyra Press, 2019). She is also the author of *The Unknowable Mystery of Other People, Personal Astronomy, When You Escape, Insectomania,* and *Arithmetic and other verses,* as well as the editor of a poetry anthology, *Joys of the Table.* Zakariya blogs at www.butdoesitrhyme.com.

Gyroscope Press
PO Box 1989
Gillette, WY 82717
gyroscopepress@gmail.com

www.ingramcontent.com/pod-product-compliance
Lightning Source LLC
Chambersburg PA
CBHW051704040426
42446CB00009B/1303